Patience

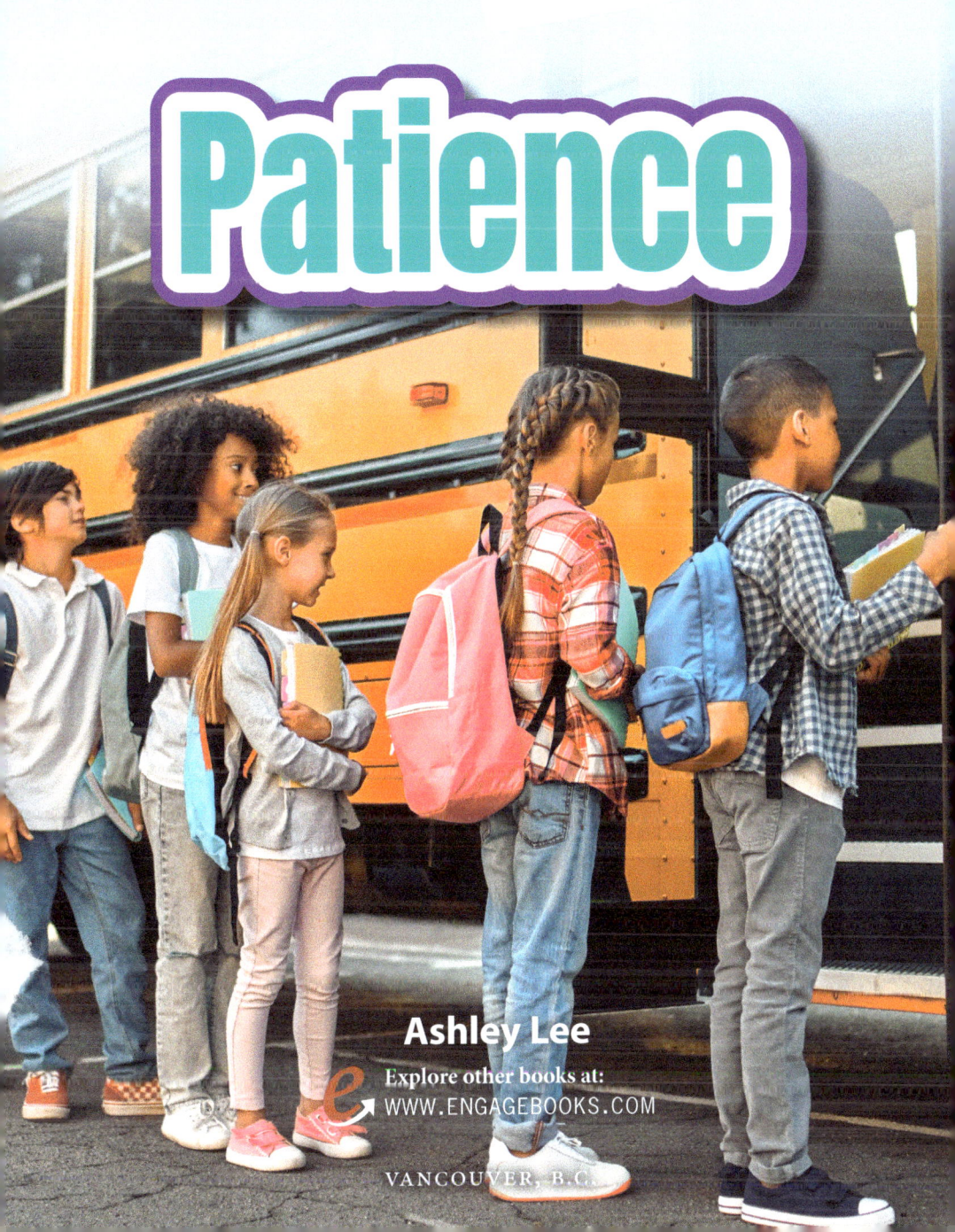

Ashley Lee

Explore other books at:
WWW.ENGAGEBOOKS.COM

VANCOUVER, B.C.

WWW.ENGAGEBOOKS.COM

Patience: Good Character Traits
Lee, Ashley, 1995 –
Text © 2024 Engage Books
Design © 2024 Engage Books

Edited by: A.R. Roumanis
Design by: Mandy Christiansen

Text set in Myriad Pro Regular.
Chapter headings set in Anton.

FIRST EDITION / FIRST PRINTING

All rights reserved. No part of this book may be stored in a retrieval system, reproduced or transmitted in any form or by any other means without written permission from the publisher or a licence from the Canadian Copyright Licensing Agency. Critics and reviewers may quote brief passages in connection with a review or critical article in any media.

Every reasonable effort has been made to contact the copyright holders of all material reproduced in this book.

LIBRARY AND ARCHIVES CANADA CATALOGUING IN PUBLICATION

Title: Patience / Ashley Lee.
Names: Lee, Ashley, author.
Description: Series statement: Good Character Traits

Identifiers: Canadiana (print) 20230446973 | Canadiana (ebook) 20230446981
ISBN 978-1-77878-667-9 (hardcover)
ISBN 978-1-77878-668-6 (softcover)
ISBN 978-1-77878-669-3 (epub)
ISBN 978-1-77878-670-9 (pdf)

This project has been made possible in part by the Government of Canada.

Canada

Patience

Contents

- 4 What Is Patience?
- 6 Why Is Patience Important?
- 8 What Does Patience Look Like?
- 10 How Does Patience Affect You?
- 12 How Does Patience Affect Others?
- 14 Is Everyone Patient?
- 16 Is It Bad if You Are Not Patient?
- 18 Does Patience Change Over Time?
- 20 Is It Hard to Be Patient?
- 22 How Can You Learn to Be More Patient?
- 24 How Can You Help Others Be More Patient?
- 26 How to Be Patient Every Day
- 28 Patience Around the World
- 30 Quiz

What Is Patience?

Patience is when you stay **calm** when you are waiting for something.

Key Word

Calm: a feeling of peace or quiet.

Patience

It means not **complaining** when things do not happen quickly.

Key Word

Complaining: when someone talks a lot about how unhappy they are.

Why Is Patience Important?

Patience helps stop you from getting upset.

Patience

People are kinder when they are not upset.

What Does Patience Look Like?

Patient people wait without complaining.

Patience

They know that some things take time.

How Does Patience Affect You?

Patience helps you focus on the good things.

Patience

It makes you happier.

11

How Does Patience Affect Others?

Being patient makes other people feel calm and happy.

Patience

It shows other people how to wait calmly.

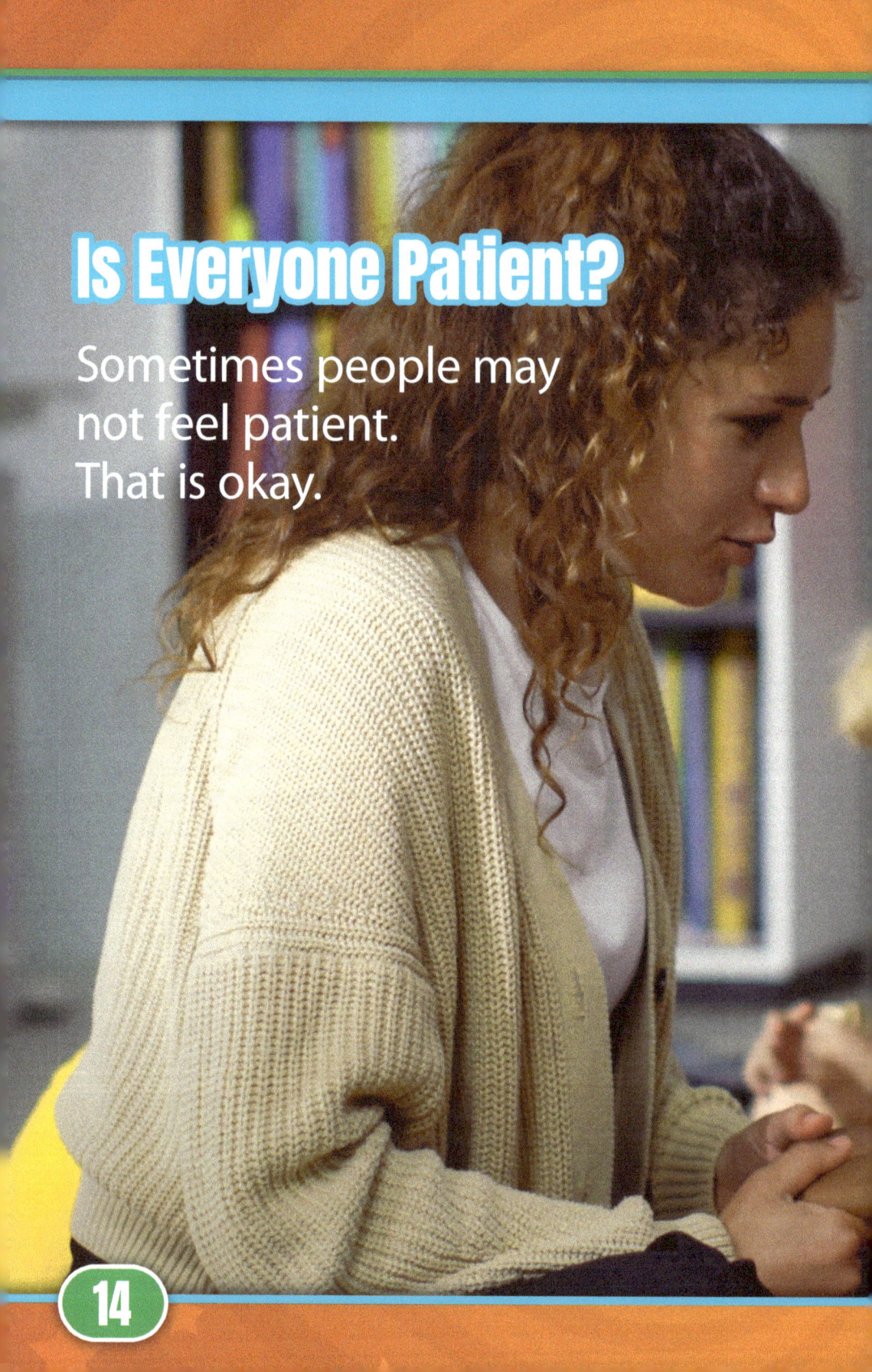

Is Everyone Patient?

Sometimes people may not feel patient. That is okay.

Patience

You should still try to stay calm when you do not feel patient.

Is It Bad if You Are Not Patient?

It is not bad if you are not always patient.

Patience

It takes time to learn to be patient.

Does Patience Change Over Time?

People often become more patient as they get older.

Patience

They learn that getting upset does not make things happen faster.

Is It Hard to Be Patient?

It can be hard to be patient if you are waiting for something **exciting**.

Key Word

Exciting: making you feel happy and full of energy.

Patience

Practicing patience can make it easier.

Key Word

Practicing: doing something over and over again so you get better at it.

How Can You Learn to Be More Patient?

Take slow, deep breaths when you feel yourself getting upset.

Patience

Practicing patience can make it easier.

Key Word

Practicing: doing something over and over again so you get better at it.

How Can You Learn to Be More Patient?

Take slow, deep breaths when you feel yourself getting upset.

Patience

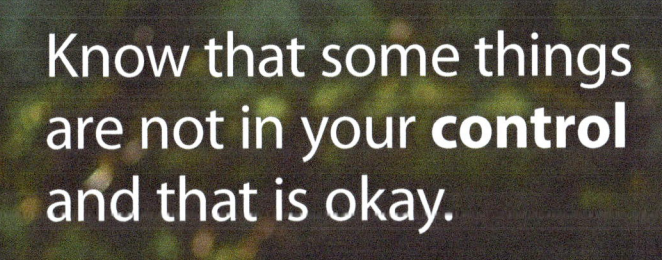

Know that some things are not in your **control** and that is okay.

> **Key Word**
> **Control:** in charge of something.

23

How Can You Help Others Be More Patient?

Play a game or tell a story.

24

Patience

This can help take their mind off of what they are waiting for.

25

How to Be Patient Every Day

1. Focus on what you are doing, not what is coming.
2. Take deep breaths.

Key Word

Focus: pay attention.

Patience

3. Know that you have to wait sometimes.

4. Try not to be in a hurry all the time.

Patience Around the World

It takes a long time for food to grow.

Patience

People all over the world have to be patient while they wait for things to grow.

Quiz

Test your knowledge of patience by answering the following questions. The questions are based on what you have read in this book. The answers are listed on the bottom of the next page.

1 Does patience help stop you from getting upset?

2 Do patient people complain while they wait?

3 Does patience make you happier?

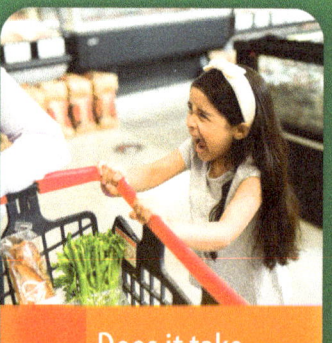

4 Does it take time to learn to be patient?

5 Does getting upset make things happen faster?

6 Can practicing patience make it easier?

30

Explore Other Pre-1 Readers.

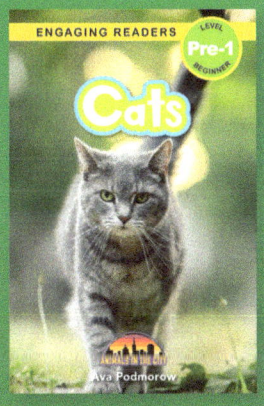

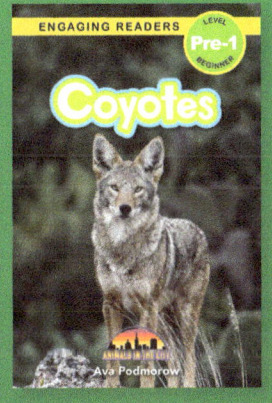

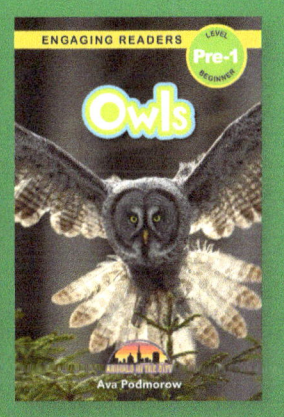

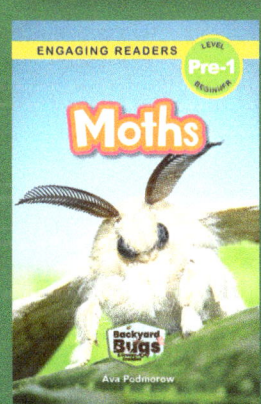

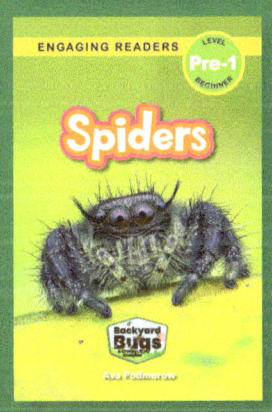

Visit www.engagebooks.com/readers

Answers: 1. Yes 2. No 3. Yes 4. Yes 5. No 6. Yes

Milton Keynes UK
Ingram Content Group UK Ltd.
UKHW051106141024
449707UK00017B/199

9 781778 786686